HUNTING AND FISHING

in Ancient Australia

R.T. Watts

KNOWLEDGE
BOOKS AND SOFTWARE

10

Teacher Notes:

Australia's First Nations people survived for so many thousands of years by developing successful hunting and fishing methods. This story discusses the challenges they faced, including dealing with megafauna and changing climates. It also demonstrates their ability to problem solve and work as a team to ensure their survival as well as the survival of their environment. By caring for country, the country cared for them.

Discussion points for consideration:

1. Discuss examples of how the First Nations people relied on the land and the sea for their survival.

2. How did our First Nations people use teamwork, creativity and technology to hunt and catch their food?

3. Why do you think Megafauna existed in these times? Why do you think they died out?

4. How did our First Nations people care for country? Why was this so important?

Sight words, difficult to decode words, and infrequent words to be introduced and practised before reading this book:

Australia, Europeans, Victoria, Tasmania, protein, vitamins, Keto, athletic, practising, woomera, dugong, billabongs, oysters, middens, Macadamia, Queensland, antioxidants, ancient, extinct, Diprotodon, Thylacoleo, Genyornis.

Acknowledgement of the First Nations' People: We acknowledge the Traditional Owners of country throughout Australia and recognise their continuing connection to land, waters and culture. We pay our respects to their Elders past, present and emerging.

Contents

1

1. Introduction

The First Peoples of Australia lived in Australia for over 60,000 years before Europeans. This is a long time, which means they knew how to survive and thrive.

The First Nations People were in all parts of Australia. There were desert people, the river people of southern Australia, and other nations in Tasmania.

They were able to hunt and collect foods from their country. In the time you may spend going to school, they had found their food for the day. They had time for art, music and having fun.

European people sometimes saw Australia as a very harsh place. It did not have any of the foods that they ate. But for the First Nations people, food was all around them. The foods had protein from low fat animals, vitamins from the plants, and energy-rich yams and fruits. Today, people call that sort of diet a "Keto diet".

The great explorers and sea captains saw the First Nations people as strong, athletic types. They ate well and lived very active lives. How humans live now is very different to those times.

2. Plenty of Food

The First Nations people did not have to move very far to find food.

The ground was dug using sharp sticks. In the ground you could find big yams in many parts of Australia. The ground also had grubs from trees, and other animals living below the ground. You had to know where to look and dig. The people looked for animal signs to tell them what was happening below the surface.

Women were able to collect seeds from trees and grass. These were used to make flour.

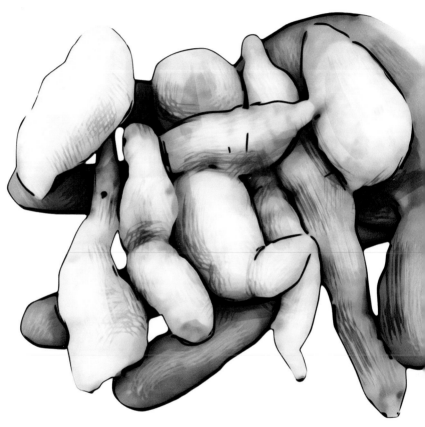

The land had many animals, big and small. The Australian animals that we see today were not the only ones. There were massive wombats as big as rhinos. There were giant emus twice the current size, and large lizards as big as crocodiles. It was a scary place to arrive a long time ago.

On the plains there were kangaroos to hunt. The people would hunt in teams and carefully sneak up on the animals. A good hunter uses a lot of care in hunting. The most important thing is to get as close as possible. The spear had a good chance of hitting if you were close to the animals.

9

If you look at the bird trapping image you can see their teamwork. The whole team would be scaring the ducks. The ducks will be pushed into the nets.

There's a better chance of success hunting with a team, than when hunting alone. As the group walks to a place to hunt animals, they may spot other animals or tracks. There are plenty of snakes, lizards and tree animals to hunt. It is a matter of spotting the animals and working out how to catch them.

3. Hunting Tools

They needed special spears and tools to hunt animals across the land and sea.

Spears were made from long pieces of wood. These were straight and strong. The spear was heated and made straight. The spear could be up to 3 metres long.

The spear had to have a sharp tip at the end. This tip could be made from stone, bone, or shell.

The tip was carefully tied and sealed with plant resin. This made a powerful spear.

It took a lot of practise to be able to throw the spear well. You had to be accurate and fast.

You could use a handle to help throw the spear. This made the spear go faster. Some First Nations people called this handle a "woomera".

There were spears for different types of hunting. When hunting small animals up close, a small spear could be used. When hunting big animals, the spear needed to be heavier.

4. Food from the Sea

There was a lot of food in the sea. All sea animals were hunted. This included fish, turtles, dugongs and birds.

Fish were caught with spears, nets, rock traps and fishing lines.

Spears were used to hunt fish off canoes. They looked down into the water and speared the fish that they could see.

Canoes were paddled out into the ocean, or the lagoon. Fish could be caught by also walking along the edge of the river or beach.

17

Traps were made to allow fish into an area. When the tide went out the fish would be caught in the trap.

Rock traps could be set up and left. Each day you could walk along and see if any fish swam into the area when the tide was high.

Reed nets could be used in lagoons, rivers and billabongs. Fish would swim into the net through the little hole. The fish could not work out how to get out.

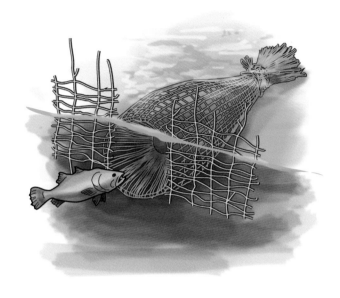

There were other foods in the sea. The sea contained shellfish, crabs and seaweed which could be eaten.

The seaweeds were used for food along with shellfish. Oysters are a form of shellfish. There were many types of food to eat from the sea.

The people would go to the seas along the coast of Australia. They would collect the shellfish. These were eaten in special places along the coast.

Today you can see large piles of these shells. These shell piles are called "middens".

There were also large mammals like whales or dugongs that could be used for food.

It was difficult to hunt whales as they were too big, and the people did not go too far off shore. If whales washed up onto the beach, they would be used for food.

Dugongs were hunted in shallow waters with spears. These were able to be speared and caught.

Turtles could be caught by diving off the canoe.

5. Food from the Land

Australia has many berries and fruits. They are not found in fruit sections of stores. But they were eaten for 60,000 years.

The common macadamia nut is now grown all over the world. This is from the rainforests in Queensland and NSW.

Finger limes are a small lime which grow in the forests. They are now being grown all over the world.

The First People knew when to come to collect these fruits and nuts. These foods are rich in vitamins and antioxidants.

Insects like moths and grubs were eaten. These were common foods from across Australia and easily found.

The trees contained all sorts of birds and lizards that could be eaten. Goanna was a big meal and would be eaten by everyone.

Birds in ponds and swamps were used for food, as well as their eggs. The people would swim under the water and grab their legs.

They could also catch the birds by scaring them into nets.

Fish and yabbies were found in the rivers. The Murray Cod was caught with nets and spears.

Birds and their eggs were eaten but you had to know where to look. The eggs were only found at certain times of the year.

A lot of wisdom about hunting had to be learned. You had to know where, when and how to hunt. Just eating one animal or plant would lead to overuse and then a shortage.

6. Megafauna

Megafauna were the ancient animals of Australia. How do we know these animals were here? The First People painted them on rocks and the walls of caves.

These were large animals which became extinct about 5,000 to 10,000 years ago.

What happened to these animals? It is not exactly known, but the end of the large animals happened about the same time the dingo arrived in Australia.

This is Diprotodon! This animal was about the size of a rhino. They ate grass and were hunted by the First Peoples.

We know it was hunted because bone pieces were found amongst ashes of a fire. It was cooked and eaten. There were cut marks on these bones from sharp stone axes used to cut the meat off the bone.

It was like a giant wombat that weighed nearly 3 tonnes.

Thylacoleo was like an Australian lion. It had powerful jaws which could break bones. It had powerful hind legs and was very strong. This meant that it was a meat eater and lived by hunting live animals.

It had long front teeth that could cut and tear meat. The long teeth could puncture the skin and cause the animal to bleed.

They were dangerous animals. You had to be careful when you were out hunting so you did not get eaten.

35

This was a large bird called Genyornis. It was hunted for the large amount of meat it could provide.

It took a team of people to hunt this bird. It was not enough to hit it with one spear. It was very dangerous to try and hunt this bird on your own. If you spotted this bird you would come back with your mates to make sure that it did not attack and kill you.

7. Caring for Country

The country looked after the First Peoples, and the First peoples looked after the country. The country was always healthy. The soil, plants and animals were never lost.

The water was clean and fresh for drinking. The rivers had fish and yabbies. The fish were always there to catch.

The land was sacred and had to be protected. This way, it always provided and always will.

This is Caring for Country!

The climate of Australia has changed over thousands of years. There are parts of Australia which are very dry and parts which are wet.

The First People saw the end of the big animals. The climate had changed, and the Ice Age ended. The forests grew in some areas and disappeared to form deserts in other areas.

As the climate and animals changed the First People moved to where the food and water could be found. New hunting and fishing areas were found. The country was still always able to feed the people.

We must continue Caring for Country if we are to live in Australia for a very long time. We must look after the animals, plants and water to make sure it is kept for everyone.

Word Bank

country	Diprotodon
Australia	protein
megafauna	macadamia
everyone	dugong
thousands	Europeans
destroyed	Tasmania
everyone	antioxidants
dangerous	ancient
powerful	extinct
Thylacoleo	protected
Genyornis	vitamins